THE CUSTOMER IS USUALLY WRONG

DISPELLING OLD MYTHS #1

OTHERWISE WE WOULD ALWAYS BE LOWERING OUR PRICE

CHUCK REAVES, CSP, CPAE, CSO

Copyright © 2015 Chuck Reaves
All rights reserved.

ISBN: 1505635667
ISBN 13: 9781505635669

TABLE OF CONTENTS

Chapter One: What Customers Really Want	1
Chapter Two: Are You Talking to the Customer?	11
Chapter Three: Are You Talking to the Customer, Part 2?	19
Chapter Four: Are You Talking to the Customer Part 3?	23
Chapter Five: Are You Talking to the Customer Part 4?	27
Chapter Six: Are You Talking to the Customer Part 5?	33
Chapter Seven: Who Is the Ultimate Customer?	37
Chapter Eight: What's the Problem?	43
Chapter Nine: What About Internal Customers?	53
Answers	67
Afterword	71

Chapter One: What Customers Really Want

"What is the fourth reason your salespeople are giving you for being unable to sell your product or service?"

That is the question I have been asking sales leaders for years as a part of the preparation for speaking at their conferences or training their salespeople. The implication in the question is that the first three reasons are obvious and ubiquitous – and they are.

Here are the first three responses I would probably hear from the salespeople in your organization in response to the question:

- Your product (or service) is inferior
- Your delivery is too slow
- Your price is too high

If the old adage, "The customer is always right", were true, you would never sell anything. The only way you could make a sale would be after you improved your product or service. Then you would need to find a way to expedite your delivery. All the while, you would need to do these things while lowering your price.

In that context, "The customer is always right" sounds a little ridiculous doesn't it?

You are not alone. If I asked that same question of your competitor's salespeople, I would hear the same response.

There are many myths in sales. The most common one is that customers buy on price. Customers have never bought on price even when we – or *they* – thought they did. They buy on perceived value – and we will address that later. The most sinister of these myths is the one that proposes that the customer is always right. There are rare instances when the customer is right about their buying criteria but they are, well, rare.

What makes this myth so troublesome is that it is one of the few that can affect everyone in your organization. The price myth affects few people outside of your sales team. After all, the folks in manufacturing or shipping may not even know what the price of your product or service is.

So if you are like most leaders you run your business on the assumption that the customer must be satisfied, delighted, overwhelmed, impressed, dazzled – or whatever word you chose at your last customer service training program. That is true; we must out-service and out-perform our competition based on the individual customer's criteria. The customer must *perceive* us to be the best in class or, at least, "the most for the money".

> We Must Out-Service And Out-Perform Our Competitors Based On The Individual Customer's Criteria.

PERCEPTION BECOMES REALITY

However, all too often the customer is incapable of knowing what they want. They may actually be asking for or demanding the wrong product or service.

What the customer actually wants is the best ***outcome***.

Customers know **what** they think they are trying to accomplish; they just may not know **how** to make it happen. In fact, they may even be wrong about what they are trying to accomplish. When that is the case, how well can they determine the best way to make it happen?

Confused?

For instance, suppose a customer has decided they want to increase their productivity by 10% so they go shopping for ergonomic furniture because they believe that's the best way to achieve that outcome. What if you sold a software program that would increase their productivity by 20%? The customer would have been low-balling their outcome potential and they would be looking at the wrong resources.

Chapter 1: What Customers Really Want

"THE SINGLE, MOST IMPORTANT FUNCTION OF SALES IS TO TEACH." – CHUCKISM #15

Professional salespeople teach. The image of the "typical" salesperson is not a pretty one nor is it one the majority of sales professionals deserve. Some people who claim to be in sales may persuade, cajole, intimidate or scare their customers. The stereotypical salesperson is seen as using these types of tactics.

However, the sales professional knows that when a customer understands the value of what they are selling, the customer buys from them. So professionals take the time to learn what their customer is trying to achieve (their desired outcome). Once they understand their customer's desired outcome, they teach the customer how their product or service will address the issue and benefit the customer. The educated customer then buys. They are not sold, they buy.

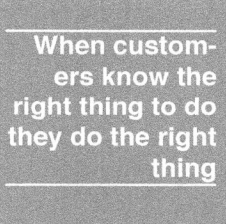

When customers know the right thing to do they do the right thing

Or, as Oprah puts it, *"When we knew better, we did better."* When customers know the right thing to do, they do the right thing.

So what have your salespeople been teaching your customers?

Let's take a closer look at the three most common objections.

"YOUR PRODUCT OR SERVICE IS INFERIOR"

Have your salespeople been teaching your customers that your competitor's offering is superior to yours?

It's easier to do this inadvertently than we might imagine. For years we have understood that 80% of selling happens at the subconscious or subliminal level. Our communication is affected by our choice of words, intonation in our voices, body language and a host of other factors. Recent studies have raised that number to 93%. We can easily and inadvertently communicate the wrong information to our customers.

If we hear something often enough we are likely to believe it. If you were out selling and several times each day you heard someone say that your competitors' offerings are superior to yours, you might begin to believe it. That is what is happening to your salespeople.

The Customer is Usually Wrong

When the customer says your product or service is inferior, the way your salespeople respond is a teaching moment.

1. Do they apologize for the inadequacy of your offering? If they believe that the competitor's offering is superior, they will inadvertently communicate that. If they say something like, "Yes, we are looking into adding that feature…" then they are validating the customer's assumption that the competition is superior. A better response is something like, "Our customers have found that our approach works better for them."
2. Do they downplay the superiority of the competition's offering? We cannot win by putting down someone else. Also, if we say that the competition's product is not as good as the customer thinks it is, have we insulted the customer?
3. Do they come back to the leadership in your company and complain that they need for the product or service to be upgraded?

Or, as professionals, do they patiently take the time to teach the customer how your product or service helps them achieve their desired outcome despite the lack of bells and whistles offered by the competition?

Doesn't this also mean that *your* product or service is different from the competition's? Are your customers demanding that your competitors meet *your* differentiation as well?

Hmmm.

If you have features A, B and C and your competitor has features B, C and D, your customers may use D as your shortcoming. "Your competition is better – they have D," they will say and your salesperson may come back to you and tell you that the only way they can sell is for you to add D to your feature list.

Meanwhile, the same customer is telling your competitor that you have A and since they do not, *your* product or service is superior! The competitor's salesperson will likely run to their leadership team and demand that A be added to *their* feature list.

A sales professional will know their competitors. This means they will know the strengths and weaknesses of the other options the customer is considering. They learn how to sell around the perceived superiority of the competition. They also learn how to sell around weaknesses their customers see in their offering.

In the scenario above, the customer may not really want D; what they want is an outcome. Is D required for your customer to achieve their desired outcome? Is it necessary?

There are no perfect products or services but every product or service can offer a near-perfect outcome.

"Your delivery is too slow"

What are your salespeople teaching your customers about the importance of timeliness?

Look at the second excuse: your delivery is too slow. So, your competition has a warehouse closer to the customer's location than you do. They can deliver faster. Or, your competitor can deliver their service faster because they have more people, more vehicles or some other capability.

Why is it in your customer's best interest that they buy from you?

The key to understanding what your customers really want and how you can best help them is found in the answer to that question. Once you can answer the question above, you will know how to proceed and your customer will have learned why they should buy from you.

In this scenario, one reason the customer may want faster deliveries is because they need to do a better job of inventory management. If they are waiting until the last minute to place their orders, you can be sure there are other weaknesses in their operations as well. An ongoing need for fast delivery is a disaster waiting to happen. After all, what if the close-by vendor is out of stock?

Is the problem delivery time or inventory management?

The delivery objection is one of many the customer could use to try and elicit concessions from your salespeople. If it wasn't delivery it might be packaging, color, credit terms or any other excuse. Because, at the end of the day, that is what it really is: an excuse.

"Your price is too high"

What are your salespeople teaching your customers about the price objection?

> The most common, most frequent objection salespeople hear is the price objection

The most common, most frequent objection salespeople hear is the price objection.

The real objection the customer is tossing out in each of the scenarios above is the price objection. The first two objections are used to put you on the defensive, soften your position and, ultimately, have you lower your price. If the buyer can degrade the perceived value of your product or service you may feel the need to lower your price.

The primary reason why customers, especially professional buyers, do this is because it works.

Over time, salespeople have taught their customers to complain about the price. Like a dog who receives a treat after performing an act, we have rewarded our customers with discounts after they performed their act of raising the price objection.

> Sales analytics enable you to be the first in your industry to raise your prices

Your price is not too high. In fact, you may want to raise it when you understand what your product or service is actually worth to your customers. This is one of the reasons why sales analytics are becoming so popular. Being able to calculate your value to your customer gives you the opportunity to be the first in your industry to raise your prices. The analytics now take on the forms of calculators, dashboards (multiple calculators) and cockpits (multiple dashboards).

If your product or service carries a higher price, a longer delivery time or lacks a feature or two your competitors have, why would your customer even give you a shot at the sale? What if your offering results in greater profit for the customer's organization? Would they be willing to wait a bit, pay more and do without some feature? Remember, buying decisions are all about outcome.

When the customer mouths the words, "Your price is too high," what are they really trying to say? It can be one of many different things such as:

- "I don't perceive the cost is equal to the value"
- "I don't think my problem is as expensive as your solution"
- "We don't need all those extra features"
- "You're no different from the competition"

You will notice that the word "price" does not appear in any of those statements.

This is why the single, most important function of sales is to teach. Sales professionals teach the customers the value of the solution they are offering.

Of course, before you can teach a customer anything you must know what to teach and the customer must be willing to learn. Determining what they want to learn is known as a needs analysis. Stimulating a desire for them to want to learn is known as an opening statement. Sales professionals do these two steps routinely. How do they develop the skills and the habits for doing this so naturally?

They understand that the customer is usually wrong.

Nobody wants what you are selling

First of all, recognize that nobody wants or needs whatever it is you are selling. Even when they contact you and say, "We want to order some of your ___" or "We need some more of your ___", your product or service is still not what they want. The customer is wrong.

> If there is a better way for your customer to achieve their outcome, they will choose it – and there's always a better way

They want what they *think* your product or service will do for them right now. The customer has a specific outcome in mind and they think your product or service will help them achieve it. If there is a better way for your customer to achieve the outcome they want, they will choose it and there is always a better way.

The Customer is Usually Wrong

Your customer buys from you for one of two reasons:

- Accomplish a goal
- Solve a problem

When they initiate the contact, they have determined that your offering can help them accomplish some objective or solve some problem. They are making this determination based on their best understanding of what you do for a living.

> Customers make buying decision based on their best understanding of what vendors do for a living

Can you keep up with all of the changes that are happening in your industry, your markets, your competitors, your technology, etc.? Probably not. If you are having trouble keeping up, what makes you think your customer is keeping up?

For instance, let's say you sell desktop computers. What if a customer contacted you and said they wanted to order some 386 computers with 20 meg hard drives and 2.5-inch floppy drives. (Some younger readers will not even know what this is. If that's you, ask someone over forty years old.) How would you respond? Would you want to say, "Hey, the 1990's called and they want their computers back?"

As absurd as this may sound, versions of this scenario happen every day. Customers order the wrong item because, to the best of their knowledge, it is the right item. They are typically using their best understanding of your capabilities and may think they are selecting the latest and the greatest solution to their problem. They do not realize a better alternative is available. And why do they not know it? It is because the salesperson has not taught them.

Remember, the single, most important function of sales is to teach.

Suppose you have three products: Small, Medium and Large. Each has its own price point and your prices in each category are all higher than your competitors' prices. A customer contacts you and asks for a quote on 1,200 Smalls. What is the customer's buying criteria? Price. You know that your competitors are going to quote prices that are lower than yours so what do your salespeople do?

1. Beg their boss for a lower price?
2. Ignore the opportunity since it is a losing proposition anyway
3. Try to determine if Small is what the customer really wants or needs

Consider scenario 1 above, *beg their boss for a lower price*. Maybe 1,200 units is a major sale for your organization and management would be willing to be "flexible" on your pricing. Flexible is another word for discounting. Being flexible on pricing rarely results in a price increase, right?

> Once we give something to a customer, it is theirs for life

Once we give something to a customer it is theirs for life. When we give them a price concession, it belongs to them from now on.

Maybe there are some economies of scale that could be used to justify a quantity discount. If that is the case then the salesperson has the responsibility to teach the customer that the justification for better pricing is higher volume.

Or consider scenario 2, *ignore the opportunity since it is a losing proposition anyway*. Why spend time responding to inquiries from customers who don't seem to appreciate how wonderful you are? After all, if a low price is all they're after, even if you fight for the sale by lowering your price you know at least one of your competitors will drop their price below yours no matter how low you go.

In scenario 3, *try to determine what the customer really wants*, it may appear that trying to determine whether or not Small is the best alternative for the customer could be a lot of work. It is – at least initially. Sales professionals develop skills and habits that actually make this type of selling faster, easier and more effective.

This type of selling is known as consultative selling, solutions selling, value-added selling, business function selling, etc. It is taught and used by thousands of the most successful companies including Fortune 500 and start-up companies. These are organizations that understand the principle that the customer is usually wrong.

The customer is seeking a successful outcome based on their best understanding of the options available to them. Some of them are unaware of just how good the best outcome could be and most are unfamiliar with at least some of the options available to them.

Instead of competing with all of the other Small sellers, why not determine how a Medium or even a Large might provide a better outcome for the customer?

Begin by determining the customer's desired outcome. Remember, this is what they think they want and may not be what they actually want to achieve. After all, the customer is usually wrong.

Suppose your Medium, which costs more than your Small of course, runs faster. Let's say it runs three times faster and costs twice as much. If your customer's desired outcome is productivity, 400 of your Mediums would do the job of 1,200 Smalls, right? And the price of 400 Mediums would equal the price of 800 Smalls rather than 1,200. Does your customer know about the capabilities of your Medium? To simplify, suppose Smalls are $1 and Mediums are $2. 1,200 Smalls would cost $1,200 but 400 Mediums would only cost $800.

This is an example of simple, basic sales analytics.

Okay, maybe we're on to something here. However, we have only begun to discuss how we can capitalize on the principle that the customer is usually wrong. There are some surprises ahead.

CHAPTER TWO: ARE YOU TALKING TO THE CUSTOMER?

All customers are not created equal. Buyers implement purchases.

In fact, most of the folks salespeople refer to as customer are not customers at all. They are buyers. There is a difference.

Some will carry the title of purchasing agent even though they are not really purchasers. They have spent their careers making buying decisions, but not purchasing decisions. They will facilitate the actual buying process of whatever someone else in their organization has decided to purchase.

These people are not making the purchasing decision: what to **buy**; they are making the buying decision: what to **pay**.

This may be a more important distinction that you think. When you ask your contact if they are the decision maker, they may yes. However, they are the decision maker only when all things are equal and they can choose between the lowest-priced alternatives.

Someone else in their organization could be setting the standards for what they will buy and your contact only makes the price decision, not the solution decision.

Most companies establish a protocol for buying. The better the protocol and the better it is followed, the better the company performs. After all, Walmart has become the successful retail behemoth because of its ability to buy, not because of its ability to sell.

The buying protocol in most companies is sort of like the mating dance we see on the National Geographic channel. In those episodes the male bird has the beautiful plumage and struts around in a strikingly flamboyant dance. His goal is to get the nod from the female bird. If birds could roll their eyes, many of the females would at this point. Scientists and

The Customer is Usually Wrong

male birds try to figure out what the female looking for – what their buying criteria is. In the corporate dance, we already know what the object of the buyer's affection is: price. The salesperson can exhibit their beautiful plumage of features, benefits, packaging, etc. but the target already has their criteria in mind. The dance may provide some entertainment and, perhaps, a some new information, but in the end, price wins.

Buyers are trying to do the right thing for their company. Any dollar they do not spend is a dollar that could make its way to the bottom line. And isn't profit what business is all about? So the buyer who shaves a dollar off of your price creates a dollar that will go to their bottom line. Buyers are sincerely trying to do the right thing for their company.

When instructed to buy 1,200 Smalls, buyers will use their corporately-endorsed, proven process of soliciting quotes from qualified sources, do their best to beat down the vendors' salespeople and will then buy the Smalls at the lowest price. If you attempt to show them the advantages of Mediums, they will respond that they are not interested in Mediums, they are buying Smalls.

Most of the time they will use a plural pronoun: "We buy Smalls here." "We have standardized on Smalls." "Don't try to change the offer, we use Smalls." Notice they are letting you know that:

1. They are not alone in the process. (This will come in handy for them later when they attempt delaying or distracting tactics.)
2. Someone else is the purchaser and is determining what to buy. The buyer is a facilitator. Purchasers are decision makers and people who make decisions like to know what options are available and might want to talk with you. Unfortunately, you're talking to a facilitator, a buyer, someone who often sees options as nuisances.

FIND SOMEONE ELSE

Someone in the client's organization would appreciate knowing about the benefits of your Medium, wouldn't they? So what do you do?

- Go around the buyer and try to find the real customer – the one who is making the purchasing decision?
- Involve the buyer in taking your story to another level?
- Give up?

Chapter 2: Are You Talking to the Customer?

The third option is never really an option. Successful salespeople persist.

The first option is dangerous. If we go around the buyer they will often retaliate later.

So let's look at the second option. Most buyers want to do the right thing for their organizations. If you were a buyer, you would likely act just as they do.

The role of every employee should be to do what they can to increase profitability. Knowingly or unaware, every employee spends their day either improving their company's financial position or harming it.

> **Knowingly or unaware, every employee spends their day either improving their company's financial position or harming it.**

When entering the workforce for the first time, some immature people will think that someone will give them a job. Employers do not give people jobs. Employers invest in resources that will generate increased profitability. Human capital is a capital investment they are willing to make because they believe there will be a positive return. Whatever position you occupy in your company, your focus should be to increase profit – the fuel companies run on.

For the buyer, the way they can contribute to the profitability of their company is to spend less for whatever they buy from you. When they spend one less dollar, that dollar can go to the company's profit. When they challenge vendors, they are trying to do the right thing for their organization.

Buyers and vendors, then, are at cross purposes. The more the vendor charges, the less successful the buyer will be – *IF* the only differentiation is price, which it never is.

> **When buyers challenge salespeople they are trying to do the right thing for their organization**

Buyers implement the purchase. Maybe we need to be talking to the purchaser.

The common wisdom among many businessmen is that there is little difference between vendors and their offerings. Therefore, companies employ someone who is better at buying than salespeople are at selling. Their vendors are funneled through the buyer's office or cubicle and only the strong survive. The strong are then thrown into the arena to battle it out to see who can lower their price the most.

Quantity vs. Quality

So why are salespeople talking to buyers?

It begins with pre-call planning. Are the salespeople asking the best questions? Instead of asking how many buyers they can call on in a week, are they asking why others in the customers' organizations would be willing to talk to them? Making a lot of calls is the old way of increasing sales – it focuses on *quantity*: "How many calls can I make?"

> Most buyers are better at buying than salespeople are at selling.

The best way to grow sales profitably is to focus on *quality*: "Who in my customer's organization will benefit most from the products/services we sell?"

When positioned with a buyer rather than a purchaser, be prepared to demonstrate how you can save the buyer's organization more money with your higher-priced offering. So how do you do that?

Price vs. Cost

You change the conversation from **price** to **cost**.

Customers are usually wrong when they ask for the lowest **price**. What they actually want is the lowest **cost**. If everything else is equal, the only differentiation between your offering and your competitor's is price. But all things are never equal.

"The only relationship that exists between cost and price is an inverse relationship." – Chuckism #39.

> "The only relationship that exists between cost and price is an inverse relationship." – Chuckism #39.

The item with the lowest price tag typically costs the most.

For instance, the lowest priced men's shirt is on the $4 table at the discount store. Why doesn't every man buy only $4 shirts?

There are multiple reasons:

- The $4 shirt will not last as long

- Will not look as good
- Will not feel as good
- Cannot be washed more than a few times
- Could harm the wearer's image

Who is supposed to teach men this message? Salespeople. The single, most important function of sales is to teach, after all.

If you are currently positioned with a buyer and want to reach the person making the purchasing decision, how will you do that?

Make the Buyer a Hero

Fighting with buyers can be like arguing with a teenager: fruitless. Is that the hill you want to fight on?

What you want is access to the purchaser. The buyer knows the purchaser. This means they know who the decision maker is, what their role or position is in their organization and, possibly, what objectives the purchaser is trying to accomplish.

So how can you encourage or entice the buyer to take you upstairs?

Two Approaches

There are two approaches: love and fear.

Using love as an approach, strive to earn the devotion of the buyer. It can be a hard pill to swallow. Making nice with someone who has been beating you up on price, putting down your product and company and telling you how inferior you are to your competitors can require some serious tongue biting.

The objective here is to assist the buyer in earning the love, admiration and respect of their organization. How is love expressed in business? Profit.

Gotta' love it!

Can you show the buyer a possibility of even greater profit?

The Customer is Usually Wrong

Since the single most important function of sales is to teach, you will want to teach the buyer that greater profitability can be realized from a different approach than can be earned from a lower price. When they embrace your approach, you have changed the dynamics of their considerations and you will often kick out the competition.

The other approach is fear. Fear of making the wrong decision has driven many buyers to seek alternatives. It can also cause paralysis by analysis so be prepared to use the cost of delaying the decision in your approach. The price objection can be an indication that the person you're talking to cannot make a decision. Additional alternatives only create more confusion, not clarity. You want to teach your contact that your offering is the safest way for your customer's organization to achieve their objective.

> Can you show your buyer the potential for greater profits?

If there is a better way to solve a problem or achieve an objective, someone in your contact's organization cares about that. You just want to find that person – or those people – and teach them what you know. Some of what you know includes the dangers and costs associated with the lower-priced alternative. This is an opportunity for you to teach.

BUYERS SELL SOMETIMES

Some buyers can sell. If you give them a reason for taking your idea upstairs, they will take it upstairs and sell it for you. So maybe you should consider your first sale to be reaching the purchaser – whoever is writing the specifications for what will be bought. What you want is access to the purchaser and your buyer may block that or facilitate it.

The purchaser wants and needs to understand the inherent inferiority of the low-priced option and the superiority of yours. Someone needs to teach the purchaser. Is that a role for you?

As with any other sale, begin with some pre-call planning.

- WIIFM – "What's In It For Me?" when "me" is the buyer. Why is it in the buyer's best interest they take you upstairs?
- Why is it in the purchaser's best interest they give you an appointment?

Chapter 2: Are You Talking to the Customer?

- How much qualifying and quantifying can you do before the call?
- What questions will you ask that will either:
    - Create fear
    - Create love

Some key words or terms you will want to use are:

- Cost-saving
- Time-saving
- New
- Advanced

The first two focus on increased profitability, the other two focus on the customer's competitive position.

To create fear, let the buyer know that you have new, relevant information that could help the purchaser make a better decision. This may be information that their competitor already has. To create love, let the buyer know that you have information that will cause their customers to buy from them more often.

Then you will need a sales plan for them to use when they go upstairs. If they are good at selling, they will benefit from your ideas. If they are not good at selling, you will need to do the selling for them. Here are some ideas:

- Put together a compelling proposition
    - Qualify why your offering is better
    - Quantify what it will do for the client's bottom line
- Offer to take the story "upstairs" for the buyer while still giving the buyer credit (this is important; the buyer must win; make the buyer a hero)
- If the buyer does not want you taking the message upstairs, package your presentation in a way that the buyer can use to take a clear and explicit message to the purchaser

The Customer is Usually Wrong

- o Use a PowerPoint
- o Use video
- o Use an audio
- o Have a landing page on your web site buyers can use to teach purchasers

Be creative. Be as specific to each customer's needs as possible. Give the purchaser as many reasons as you can to spend time with you. Purchasers usually have more reasons and time to consider alternatives than buyers.

So, the buyer is not the customer. It does not matter if they are right or wrong; let's move on to the purchaser's office…

CHAPTER THREE: ARE YOU TALKING TO THE CUSTOMER, PART 2?

All customers are not created equal. Purchasers determine purchases.

Somewhere in the bowels of the company there is someone who is responsible for learning your business. That's right; they learn your business for the purpose of deciding whether or not they should buy what your company offers. If they decide that what you sell is right for them, they will instruct the buyer to solicit offers from everyone they can find who sells what you sell. This is done in obscurity and you will rarely know what other alternative vendors are being considered.

Of course if they cannot find you, you will not be in the game. Every day that passes someone buys from one of your competitors without even considering you. Is that the right thing to do? Of course not; the customer is usually wrong. Why are they not considering you? Is it because you have not taught them that you exist? Marketing takes the primary responsibility for making prospects aware of your existence. However, as a sales professional you are also accountable for introducing yourself to potential buyers.

When the buyer contacts you, don't feel too special. They are also looking at many other businesses and industries. And there are usually multiple purchasers in your buyer's organization. As important as you may think you are, you are competing with people you probably don't know and you may not even know they exist.

Businesses buy solutions. If you sell nails and the business is using glue as their solution, you may not know they are shopping. Even when you know they are looking for a vendor, their mindset may be, "We buy glue." But what if nails would offer a better alternative? You would be competing with glue companies – and what do you know about glue, glue companies and glue salespeople? You must know your competitor whether they are in the same industry or not.

The Customer is Usually Wrong

Purchasers are looking for the best solution; buyers are looking for the lowest price. The purchaser's objective is to find as many ways as possible to improve their company's bottom line. If they have been buying glue for many years, they will know glue. When you show up to sell them nails, they will quickly tell you that they buy glue.

Here is where it can become complicated. What if the purchaser who buys nails is down the hall from the purchaser who buys glue? Sometimes purchasers compete internally for the available dollars. Now the sale is getting really difficult. If the nail purchaser is not as persuasive as the glue purchaser, their organization may focus on glue instead of nails.

Maybe you should just go find nail purchasers – and drop your price.

There could be an alternative. In our glue/nail example, what are we really talking about?

Fasteners.

The customer organization is trying to affix two items together. If they use glue and you're in the nail business, they are not a customer. However, if you are in the fastener business, you've got a shot.

What Business Are You In?

You need to answer this question frequently because the answer changes. As your markets change, so does your answer. As your technologies change, so does your answer. As your capabilities change, as you upgrade your existing line and add new lines the answer changes.

The business you're in determines which purchaser you should be talking to.

As an example, what business are these companies in?

- McDonalds
- Costco
- Lauterbach Printing

If you answered food, retail and printing then, like most folks do, you are three for three wrong. McDonalds is in the real estate business, Costco

Chapter 3: Are You Talking to the Customer, Part 2?

is in the membership business and Lauterbach is in the ink-on-substrate business.

The success rate of McDonalds' restaurants can be traced to their ability to pick great locations. Using sophisticated data, analysis, algorithms and other tools they continuously update, they have prime real estate wherever they are located.

If you examine the financials for the clubs like Costco you will see that their net profit is nearly equal to their revenue from membership fees. Their goal is to increase the number of new members and renewals every year.

These two giants, McDonalds and Costco, can afford to have brilliant teams of people working together to figure these things out. But what about a more typical organization, one closer to the one you probably work for?

Look at Lauterbach, a second generation, family-owned printing business in the Milwaukee area. The patriarch began the business printing labels and they became known as one of the best label printers in the country. Their claim to fame was quality, service and timeliness. Their primary market was printing return address labels for non-profit organizations who used the labels for fundraising. Remember when you used to receive an envelope full of return address labels and a request for a donation in return? Have you received one recently?

Technology changed their target market. Email replaced snail mail. They began asking "who else" and "what else". Who else could benefit from their capabilities? What else could they do for their existing clients?

Lauterbach is one of the fortunate few in their industry for whom technology is a blessing, not a threat. They had already invested in the latest technologies associated with printing as well as developing their own state-of-the-art recycling and sustainability programs and technologies.

> **Regularly ask the questions:
> Who else?
> What else?**

As long as they were printing labels for non-profits, their days were numbered. However, when they considered putting ink on various substrates, the world opened up. They pioneered a new technology in tamper-proof labels for bottles. They found a way to make a label that will talk to your smartphone. They can make an interactive direct mail piece for those clients still using snail mail! They found numerous ways of helping their customers sell better, faster and at a lower cost.

Where they once spent most of their teaching time with buyers for non-profits who beat them up on price, they are now engaging purchasers at all levels of many different organizations in multiple industries. They talk to marketing people who are reallocating budgets from other areas to the ink-on-substrate industry and Lauterbach in particular.

Learn from their approach. For clients sticking to snail mail, they are fine-tuning the familiar. For others, they are redefining the offering.

Someone else out there needs what your organization produces. Can you find the purchasers who will understand what you have to teach? What business are you in?

The Purchaser

Hold on a minute. Is the purchaser the customer? If so, which purchaser?

Remember that there are usually multiple purchasers in the customer's organization. If the organization cannot fund every purchaser's request, who makes the final decision?

> When is it time for you to fine-tune the familiar and when is it time for you to redefine the process?

If your nail purchaser is competing for budget dollars with the glue purchaser, can *they* sell your offering upstairs?

So who controls that aspect of our sales? Who else do you need to be teaching? Usually it's someone in finance.

CHAPTER FOUR: ARE YOU TALKING TO THE CUSTOMER PART 3?

All customers are not created equal. Financial people approve purchases.

Even when the buyer and the purchaser are convinced, the sale can still be lost to a more compelling story at another level.

If you are selling widgets that will increase productivity in manufacturing and the folks in Administration desperately need new office furniture, which will your client purchase?

I once lost a sales training contract to GMC trucks. The customer told me our agreement was a done deal and the customer was wrong. At the last minute the "sure thing" turned into "not now". It turns out that the customer's fleet was causing a reduction in revenue due to failures in delivery and was also draining profits with ongoing repairs. When the VP of sales and the VP of operations made their cases for funding, operations won.

It was the right call. You don't want your salespeople selling more when your ability to deliver is weak. It only frustrates customers and salespeople.

TEACHING THE BEAN COUNTER

Generally speaking, salespeople don't do numbers. How can we understand our proposition well enough to educate someone in finance?

What do you teach a financial person? Here's a hint, the fact that your service includes a twenty-four hour hotline will not interest the numbers person. They won't be calling the hotline. The fact that your new widget "puts twenty-four volts on pin 6 of the main connector" will not interest the financial buyer. They aren't into voltage. The engineers and manufacturing people might be excited about it but for the numbers guy, it won't mean much.

Finance people speak finance, which is a strange language to most of us salespeople. Generally speaking, we don't do numbers.

If a salesperson designed an expense report, how many boxes would it have? The answer is two: Name and Total.

Since the green eye shade people have veto power over the funding of your sale, perhaps you need to learn to speak their language. Successful people know what they don't know and then they find people who are strong in their weak areas. If finance is a weakness for you, ask for help.

Sales analytics was created to address this issue. More and more organizations are developing calculators to demonstrate the positive ROI results of using their offering. They are combining multiple calculators into dashboards and then melding dashboards into cockpits. These comprehensive tools help the customer calculate the impact of their purchase with greater and greater accuracy.

> When is it time for you to fine-tune the familiar and when is it time for you to redefine the process?

With these tools, salespeople do not necessarily need an in-depth understanding of financial principles. The tools can do most of the work – the heavy lifting – for the salesperson who is teaching a financial buyer.

One consumer products company developed an interactive calculator their retailers could use. They could enter and adjust data to run what-if analyses. The supporting data came from industry sources and the algorithms were clearly explained. In the worst case, the retailers typically saw an ROI of less than three months. The buyers were convinced without really knowing the details of the product. What they understood was how the product performed financially in the marketplace. That's all they needed to know. The fact that the product used a better aloe was of no interest to them. Once they saw that reallocating a few shelf inches would result in a six-figure rise in profits, the decision became a no-brainer.

Tools like this are intellectual candy for many financial buyers.

By the way, in this case the buyer in the retail organization saw no use for the calculator and purchasers also passed it up. The financial folks became the champions.

Chapter 4: Are You Talking to the Customer Part 3?

Jim Franklin became the CEO of a software company in Denver after serving as the CFO for another successful software company. He held Saturday tutoring session sessions for his salespeople and taught them how to read a 10K, a 10Q, financial statements and other resources financial people seem to find to be interesting.

It worked. Cost justifications at his company become increasingly sophisticated and they increased in frequency. When salespeople know the right thing to do they do the right thing. So, sales leadership needs to be in the teaching mode as well.

When the financial person is your contact, what will you teach them?

The difference in the teaching process at this level as compared to the buyer level is the difference in elementary school and college.

Many buyers are becoming increasingly sophisticated. They understand the difference in cost and price. They will challenge the higher-priced vendor with, "what are we getting for the extra dollars," rather than, "your price is too high". Once the vendor explains the differentiation, these sophisticated buyers are excellent at explaining the cost benefits to their superiors. As a result, they do not remain buyers very long. They move upstairs and often join the financial team.

By the time they reach the upper levels where strategic buying decisions are made, they have experienced many different vendor scenarios. Their opinions and ideas are valuable. So, rather than teaching them by the "show up and throw up" method, it is time for a sophisticated interactive teaching moment. Just remember that you will have at least as much to learn as you will have to teach.

They will get deep into the financial weeds quickly, if you let them. If that is where they want to talk, consider taking someone from your organization who understands numbers with you. Otherwise, focus your teaching on the solution, not the details.

Begin by learning their objectives – most of which will be given to you in financial terminology. Ask them what information they would like to see from you and in what format they would like for you to deliver it.

Recognize that no matter how comprehensive your numbers may be, they may still want more. That's just the way it is with these analytic types;

they enjoy having more stuff to analyze. And even though they may appear to be dissatisfied with your delivery, they will appreciate the fact that you are trying.

Once the numbers person is convinced, they will become your advocate, your champion. Remember in your sales training when you were taught to find a champion in the customer's organization? There is no better champion than the bean counter. Their conclusions are usually iron clad.

And they can be wrong. After all, the customer is usually wrong.

While they are masters at finding the best and most profitable path for achieving the corporate objective, what if they are wrong about the objective? What if you have thoroughly cost justified a higher-priced plane ticket to Chicago but the customer is going to Boston?

Focus on outcome, destination or however the client's organization defines success. Success is a destination.

Who knows where the company is going? The customer's leader knows and their point of view is different from anyone else in their organization.

CHAPTER FIVE: ARE YOU TALKING TO THE CUSTOMER PART 4?

All customers are not created equal. Leaders determine destinations.

What we have seen so far is:

- Buyers implement purchases
- Purchasers determine purchases
- Financial people approve purchases

Now we go to the next level: purpose. What is the purpose of the purchase? What is your buyer's organization trying to accomplish? Where are they trying to go?

If you look at your customer's organization chart, you will typically see one lone box at the top. That's the leader. It may be the Chairman, President, CEO or some other title, and it is where the proverbial buck stops. The onus is on that individual to determine where the organization will be in the future. It is not an easy or enviable position.

Compare it to an airline captain. The captain knows the destination and can chart a course based on the information available at the time. However, while in flight, weather, ground stops, ATC holds and other unforeseen events can alter even the most detailed plan.

Depending on their industry and the markets they serve, the leader may be developing plans for six, twelve, twenty-four or even forty-eight months out. After all, someone has to determine where the organization will go and how to get there.

Meanwhile, they are held accountable for the immediate monthly or quarterly results. The short-term accomplishments (or lack of them) are the result of the planning they did six, twelve, twenty-four or forty-eight months ago.

How do they chart the course?

Like the airline captain, they gather the best information available at the time and chart a course. The primary source of information for the typical leader is their strategists, the occupiers of the C-Level. This would include the CFO, the COO, the CIO/CTO and, increasing, the Chief Sales Officer, the CSO.

You have probably noticed that buyers and purchasers are not included in this inner circle.

How?

The leader asks "how" questions. They do not ask if something can be done or should be done. Based on their involvement in industry associations, leadership organizations as well as the reading they do and the seminars they attend, they know what the destination needs to be. All they need to know is how to get there.

This applies to high-growth companies as well as companies struggling to stay afloat.

Two lines from the movie "Apollo 13" are used frequently at the leadership level. "Houston we have a problem," is the first. Every organization has problems and leaders are problem solvers.

There are two types of problems: those that keep an organization down and those that prevent the organization from going higher. Weak cash flow can hold a company down while insufficient floor space can keep an organization from growing. Both are problems and both can be solved by multiple alternatives.

What you want is for the leader in your buyer's organization to consider your offering as the primary solution.

Jeff Cook runs an engineering company that specializes in hotel electronic infrastructure. He has clients and competitors. However, it is not unusual for a client, a hotel company, to call and ask him to send some-

Chapter 5: Are You Talking to the Customer Part 4?

one out to show them what options are available. There is no question about who they will buy from; the only question is what specific configuration they will buy from Jeff's company.

The second line is, "Failure is not an option". They will fight to the bitter end to reach the destination they know is best for their organization.

The analysis of black box recordings from major airline disasters show that right until the moment of impact, the captain and first officer were looking for alternative solutions. Nothing describes the mental process of a leader better than that.

So how do you get in to the CEO's office?

You probably don't nor do you need to in most cases. What you want is to understand the destination, the objective the leader believes the organization must achieve. Armed with that knowledge, you will want to determine what you can do to help.

AT&T sent me to Acapulco as a reward for being their top salesperson. When I returned they applied the Peter Principle and made me a sales manager, a National Account Manager, NAM, to be specific. AT&T had 256 national accounts and two of them needed managers: number 13 and number 256. Which one would you pick?

I took number 256 because the only way it could go was up. When I accepted the position, the company started a clock. I had ninety days to meet face-to-face with the client's CEO or I was to consider myself unemployed. That was the rule for anyone accepting a NAM position.

To be a national account, the customer's phone bill had to exceed $2,000,000 a month. These were not small companies. We were taught how to make our way into the CEOs' offices. We had to know what their objectives were, what obstacles they were facing and what their competitors were up to. Fortunately, in a huge company like that, most of the information was publically available.

The CEO of my national account had two lawsuits against AT&T, my employer. One stated that we were aggressively trying to put them out of business, which we were. They were an emerging threat known as resellers. The second was an injunction that forbade us from going into his building. We had our work cut out for us.

After a lot of time and effort trying to build trust, respect and a mutually-agreeable relationship, the CEO called me into his office and said, "We will give you [this major project] if you will get me an audience with Arch McGill. Mr. McGill was the sales and marketing genius that had turned around IBM and was in the process of turning AT&T into a powerhouse. The CEO wanted someone of that caliber to apologize for how AT&T had treated his company.

I cashed in every chip I had on my side of the table from having been the top salesperson and managed to put together the meeting. It was amazing. Both men were Olympic-quality corporate game players. They were using positioning tactics I had never even heard of.

McGill allowed my customer to download his complaints and when the CEO took a breath, McGill would ask, "And what else?" The CEO would see that as an open door and unload some more.

When the CEO seemed to have exhausted the bulk of his tirade, McGill said, "I don't like this any more than you do. But if it's not a billion dollars, it does not cross my desk."

My customer's $50 million phone bill would not show up on McGill's radar. Some people think $50 million is not a lot of money.

Your sales will likely not show up on your customer's leader's radar. They probably see no reason for you to interact directly with them. You may not need to. You just need to understand "destination". Where is the buyer's organization trying to go and what can you do to help them get there?

No More Account Penetration

If you have had consultative selling or solution selling training, you were probably taught the concept of account penetration. The idea is to go as high as you can in the customer's organization. As you have seen, when you go higher you find people who are interested in outcomes. They want to know what you can deliver and how it can impact their objectives not just what you charge.

Think instead of account saturation. How many quality relationships can you have in your key accounts? This is the secret to consultative selling or solution selling.

> **Think account saturation, not penetration**

Chapter 5: Are You Talking to the Customer Part 4?

There are two reasons why you want to have multiple relationships: multiple perceptions and competitive prevention. We cannot do consultative selling by talking to just one person. And, if your competition ever comes nosing around your account, you want to already be positioned with whoever they contact.

Think triangulation. The most stable platform is a tripod. Milk stools have three legs so they will sit steadily regardless of the terrain beneath them. Your GPS needs a minimum of three satellites to give you directions. You need at least three contacts in your customer's organization.

Even if you could spend time with the CEO, you would still be hearing only one perspective. Granted it would be a high-level perspective, but still only one. So you need at least three.

Over the years I have asked hundreds of CEOs and other senior executives what their top three problems were. None of them have ever told me – not one!

My first consulting client said his top problem was attrition. When I asked him what his attrition rate was for the previous year he answered 112%! He had turned over the equivalent of his entire employee base more than once in only a year.

Was attrition his problem? Nope.

It was a symptom. What was driving the turnover?

Your customer's CEO has explained the corporate direction to the leadership team. Interview three of them and you will probably hear three different perspectives of the goals and three different approaches for achieving them. What can you do to bring them all together?

> **Whenever two minds come together, a third mind is created**

The longer you use consultative or solution selling, the more competent you will become in finding ways to unravel the problems they are facing. You will be able to look past the symptoms in order to see the problems. You will be able to ask better questions.

You will also capitalize more effectively on the fact that whenever two minds come together, a third mind is created. The best solution is usually in that third mindset. .

The Customer is Usually Wrong

If the customer is not the buyer, the purchaser, the financial person or the leader, who is?

Think Supply Chain Selling.

CHAPTER SIX: ARE YOU TALKING TO THE CUSTOMER PART 5?

All customers are not created equal. Who is your customer's customer?

In a business-to-business, B2B, world, we don't sell to, we sell through.

How many of your customers have taken one of your products and put it on a pedestal in the lobby of their building so that all of their customers can see that they buy from you?

General Motors may be buying the best shock absorbers made. But when you go into the lobby of their buildings, you will see beautiful automobiles, not shock absorbers.

Instead of looking at your customer, think about your customer's customers. What would it take to cause your customer's customers to buy more from your customer's organization?

This is Level 2 of Supply Chain Selling. In Level 1 we saturate the customer's organization and build as many relationships as we can. Now we look down the customer's supply chain.

Right now, while you are reading this, what is your customer probably thinking about?

- Your product or service?
- The great presentation you made the last time you were out there?
- Your price?
- The wonderful unique features of your offering
- How they can sell more of their products or services to their customers?

The answer is obvious, so what can you do to help your customer sell more?

The Sales VP for a technology company recently sent me an email. We have been working on teaching their salespeople to open the sales call by talking about the customer, not their killer technology. It seems he accompanied the rep on a sales call to Mars Candy. Mars was in the process of sorting through all of the companies that provide the same type of technology and Mars was hearing pretty much the same thing from each. When the rep stood up, one of their customers leaned back in his chair with his arms folded and bellowed, "What have YOU got for us?"

Without hesitation the rep said, "I'm here to help you sell more chocolate".

Before, a thirty-minute presentation would have included twenty five minutes of an elaborate PowerPoint presentation about the vendor's technology. This would have been exciting for the rep and ho-hum for the customer. Instead, the bulk of the time was spent talking about how Mars wanted to attract a new generation of customers.

Mars does not really care what any of its vendors do – they care about what their customers do. Then they look for ways their vendors can help them sell more effectively to folks who want a quality chocolate treat.

Who is your customer's customer? What can you do to help?

Then, who is your customer's customer's customer? We're looking further down the customer's supply chain now.

For instance, if your customer sells through distribution, what do you know about the distributors' organizations? What do you know about their reps? Who are they calling on?

The reason you want to consider this is because it will significantly change the conversation you are having with your contacts in your customer's organization. Instead of a "oh, please buy from me" approach, you will be talking to them about their favorite topic: sales of their products and services.

In this case, the buyer's organization sells through a distributor. So what can you do to help them earn greater participation from the distributor's reps? Think about it. The distributor's reps are making sales calls –

what will they present to their prospects? If they sell multiple lines, your buyer's organization is just one of many the rep could consider. Can you help position your buyer's products or service higher in the reps' minds?

If one of your salespeople contacted me and opened with, "Mr. Reaves, we talked to your customers and here is what they told us," I would want to do business with you without even knowing what you offer. You are bringing me valuable information I do not have. Sometimes the value in value-added selling has nothing to do with what you have to sell.

Think about this. Will my accounts tell you things about me they will not tell me? Of course they will. And, will your accounts tell me things about you they will not tell you?

> Sometimes the value in your value-added selling has nothing to do with what you sell

At the bottom of your buyer's supply chain there is the ultimate source of the dollar, the USD. These are the people who are putting the money in the supply chain that everyone else is taking a piece of. The USD is usually a consumer.

When you bought your smartphone the retailer kept some of your money and then passed the remainder to a distributor. The distributor kept some of the money and passed the remainder to the manufacturer. The manufacturer kept some of the money and passed the remainder to their suppliers. We could continue examining this chain but you get the picture.

Understand how all of this works and you will be head and shoulders above your competitors. You will be better able to serve your customer, even when the customer is wrong – which they usually are.

You have heard the old adage: "Nobody cares how much you know until they know how much you care." When your accounts know how much you care, they will give you information and opportunities unavailable to your competitors.

So, who is the entity who is putting money into your account's supply chain the ultimate customer you must satisfy?

CHAPTER SEVEN: WHO IS THE ULTIMATE CUSTOMER?

All customers are not created equal. One stands alone at the top.

Like you, I have been guilty of assuming the customer was always right when, in fact, those people buying from us were usually wrong. The problem, as you will see, is the folks swapping their money for your goods and services are not the ultimate customers. The ultimate customer is not the ultimate source of the dollar in your account's supply chain. So it does really matter if they are right or wrong if our goal is to satisfy the ultimate customer – the one who is usually right.

Even though we just took a long and important look at your buyer's organization's supply chain, the ultimate customer was not on there.

Your ultimate customer is a stakeholder in your organization.

This is a major shift in thinking for many of us. Thinking of your boss as "the customer who must be pleased" is 180 degrees out of phase for most people. As you will see, being able to please that person will result from your being able to please everyone else – including those folks you have been referring to as customers – any of those buyers in your supply chain.

What if your ultimate customer is the CEO of your organization? What would their buying criteria be? In most situations it would look like this:

- Increased revenue
- Increased profit
- Increased market share

It's pretty simple and easy to remember. It is not easy to accomplish, as you know.

There are exceptions, of course. Some start-up companies know that profitability will have to wait as they work to create a revenue stream. Other organizations are niche players and only want certain segments of the market. Generally speaking, however, the way to a CEO's heart is through revenue, profit and market share.

> Pleasing the customer is simple, it just isn't easy

Ultimate Customer Satisfaction

Pleasing a CEO is simple; it just isn't easy.

When the buyer tells you that your price is too high, lowering your price will cause you to miss two of your ultimate customer's criteria, won't it? Revenue and profit will inevitably be lower. But you will be increasing your market share. Shouldn't one out of three be enough? Of course it will not.

In the heat of the moment, when it seems that a sale <u>absolutely</u> hinges on some concession the buyer is demanding, how easy is it to capitulate, give in and close the deal? In the back of your mind you may be thinking that forgiveness is easier than permission and at least you will be bringing some revenue to your company. It may not have the same profitability that your ultimate customer wants, but it's something. After all, it will contribute to one of your ultimate customer's objectives: market share.

Salespeople often have a cushion, a buffer that protects them from the dissatisfaction or wrath of the ultimate customer. It's known as a sales manager, vice president of sales or other similar title. They can bring their discounted sale to their manager who will then have to explain to the ultimate customer why they will not be receiving what is wanted: increased revenue, increased profit and increased market share.

Sales leaders like sales managers and vice presidents, do a disservice to their salespeople when they fight their battles for them. Sales leaders who came up through the ranks may have a desire to "help" their subordinates by apologizing to the ultimate customer for them. These are the sales leaders that think they need to make sales calls for their salespeople.

Chapter 7: Who Is the Ultimate Customer?

As a National Account Manager for what was then the largest company in the world, AT&T had expectations of my performance. I was given a set of objectives and an account team. We had the highest price, oldest technology and slowest delivery. Other than that we were pretty darned competitive.

When the Account Executives on the team would come to me and tell me that our price prevented them from making their sales – and subsequently their quotas – I made a deal with them. They had to show me six different approaches they had used to try and close each account. If their customer was still unwilling to buy, I would add their quota to mine – something the company did not allow.

None of them ever brought me a lost sale. By the time they made the third or fourth attempt, they had uncovered the real problems their account was facing and had offered a quantified solution. This became a win-win-win.

Bad News Travels Like Wildfire

Seasoned sales managers develop a knack for delivering bad news. When the buyer or purchaser has to hear some bad news, astute sales managers will go out and deliver the message so that the sales rep is not associated with the delivery of the unappreciated message. It helps the rep maintain their positioning with the buyer. Seasoned sales managers are also the lamb that sometimes goes to the slaughter in meetings with the leadership team. When salespeople underperform, sales managers find themselves on the carpet, not the sales rep.

So, often, it is the sales leader who is delivering the bad news to the ultimate customer, the stakeholder.

Which Stakeholder?

Your ultimate customer is the stakeholder in your organization who has the most to gain or lose with the company's successes and failures. The ultimate customer has expectations. Those expectations must be met or there will be consequences. On the other hand, when those expectations are exceeded, there will be rewards, sometimes generous rewards, spread around.

These rewards can vary in value from continued employment to financial rewards to promotions. So it is in everyone's interest to satisfy this ultimate customer. And, it is in the interest of many to go <u>beyond</u> satisfying them.

Corporate objectives are established based on the expectations of the ultimate customer. If the CEO sets the revenue growth for the upcoming year at 10%, then that's the goal everyone will need to use in setting their individual or departmental goals. If the President determines that the profit margins need to increase by 4%, then everyone needs to figure out what they can do to raise prices or lower expenses in order to increase the company's margins.

You get the idea. The primary stakeholder, the ultimate customer, lets you know what it will take to satisfy them. So, is the ultimate customer right? After all, they are your boss or your boss's boss.

Rarely. In fact, even the most astute ultimate customer is usually wrong. Here's why.

Like the buyers addressed earlier, ultimate customers make their decisions based on their best understanding of the capabilities of others. In your case they are analyzing what the sales team has communicated to them in the past. They are comparing that to the opportunities they are seeing in your market and your industry. They may also be incorporating some statistical data and analysis from multiple sources.

For instance, when they return from an industry convention or seminar, they may have indications that your organization is not growing at the same rate as others or industry norms. They may learn that others are using new technologies or processes. Despite all of the input they received from you and other members of your team, there was still some missing knowledge.

There is always missing knowledge. Technologies are changing, markets are changing –we cannot keep up.

Still, even with all of this input, they are still usually wrong.

The question we have to consider is whether or not the data being analyzed was influenced by buyers, purchasers and other people in the organizations that provided the knowledge. What if you could influence or change that? What if your sales efforts were directed at solving the problems of the folks who are sending money to your company, the ones you previously referred to as customers? And what if those folks learned that their problems were actually costing them more than they thought? Would they be willing to pay you more for your solution?

Well, that's the heart of solution selling. We determine what the problem is, we offer a solution and then we close the sale. How do we determine what the problem is? We ask that person we once referred to as a customer what their problem is.

When the customer answers, they are usually wrong. So how do you uncover the real problem?

CHAPTER EIGHT: WHAT'S THE PROBLEM?

Most customers don't know what they want.

"What are the top three problems facing your business right now?"

The question above is the most used approach in consultative or solution selling approaches. The idea is that you will ask the prospect this question and they will tell you what problems are giving them the most grief. Then, you will show them how your product or service will solve the problem and, *voila*, you have a sale.

This worked for a while until customers figured out that if your product or service would solve their problem then the lower-priced alternative from your competitor would solve the problem as well. They would thank you for your time and buy from your competitor.

A level of sophistication was added when you learned how to develop a quantified cost justification. This stopped the "shopper's mentality" in the mind of the prospect, at least for the first sale. You were convincing and got the order but by the time they were ready to buy again, the competition had shown up with their pitch: "We're the same as them only cheaper," referring to you.

None of this really matters since this is not really solution selling anyway.

In preparing for 3500 presentations all over the world I have asked my clients the question, "What are the top three problems facing your company?" Not one has ever told me. Not one. Keep in mind my contact is usually the CEO, CSO or vice president.

Remember the client who had the attrition rate of 112%? Was that a problem?

Actually, no it wasn't. What was it? It was a symptom. We needed to find the cause of the atrocious attrition rate.

Whatever answer your contact gives you to the problem question is usually wrong. After all, the customer is usually wrong, remember?

You may hear a prospect tell you that they have a recurring problem. By definition, that's a symptom.

Do not argue with your customer. Whatever they tell you the problem is, go along with it but treat it in your mind as a symptom keep looking for the root cause.

THE ROOT CAUSE

Begin by eliminating the false root causes – the ones that might have seemed like a good idea. Do this by asking your contact what they have tried in the past. There is no need to reinvent the wheel here. If they tested a solution and the symptom persists, that was the wrong solution.

In the case of the client with 112% attrition, they had tried better hiring, improving the working conditions and some other obvious remedies, none of which worked. A deeper analysis uncovered the fact that most of the attrition was entry-level employees who worked on the assembly line. These positions required only limited skills.

> Customers usually only know symptoms, not problems

Surveying the employees brought little information. Answers to questions were vanilla: "fine", "okay", "no problem".

The problem turned out to be the owner. Whenever he was having a bad day he would walk out on the production floor and find someone who was not actively doing anything, fire them on the spot and walk them out of the building. It just kind of cheered him up.

Granted, he was an old school businessman and he was not taking the time to find out why the person was not working. Sometimes the machine they were assigned to was down for maintenance or they were just returning from lunch.

Each of these episodes created fear and uncertainty in the minds of other employees who decided to look for work elsewhere.

Chapter 8: What's the Problem?

Varying vendors had offered solutions including work flow consultants, supervisor trainers, multiple equipment manufacturers and a long list of consultants. Each had focused on the symptom of attrition not realizing that the problem was the person who had hired them.

When you think you have found a solution, try this test. If your solution were to be implemented, would the "problem" go away permanently? If the answer is no, keep digging.

WHAT PEOPLE WANT

Remember, nobody wants your products or your services. Get over it. They don't want mine either. As we have seen they want an outcome, they want to reach a destination, and they think your product or service will give them that result.

What if the outcome they are seeking is wrong? After all, the customer is usually wrong.

THE HARDWARE STORE EXAMPLE

Imagine for a moment you work in a hardware store.

If a man walks into your hardware store and asks for a quarter-inch drill bit, what does he want? Here's a hint: it's not a drill bit. What he actually wants is a quarter-inch hole. They only way he knows to get his quarter-inch hole is to buy your drill bit, take it home, put it in his drill and bore the hole.

First of all, is there a better way to make a quarter-inch hole? Here's a hint: for any question that begins with "is there a better way" the universal answer is always yes. There is always a better way to do something – you just may not have found it yet.

As an example, how big is the bullet that comes out of a .22 pistol? Twenty-two one-hundredths. That's very close to twenty-five one-hundredths or a quarter-inch, isn't it? So you could make an appropriately-sized hole from across the room using this approach, right?

In this scenario, what problem is the customer trying to solve?

At this point in the sales process you don't have a clue.

You could explain the features and benefits of your quarter-inch drill bit options. You could teach the man that the carbide-tipped bits will last a very long time. You could continue to teach that the high-grade steel bits could be sharpened many times and, therefore, last a long time – and you could sell them a bit sharpener. Finally you could teach the man that you have inexpensive, throw-away bits and then move in for the close: "Which bit would you like?"

That sounds like a thorough sales presentation - it is anything but. Where in that scenario would you have learned the man's problem?

Instead, you could ask, "What project are you working on?"

Suppose the man told you that he was trying to install a ceiling fan and he had read in the instructions that he would need to drill a quarter-inch pilot hole in the ceiling joist to hold the bracket for the fan. You would have learned two important things:

1. The outcome the man was seeking (hanging the fan)
2. There were multiple opportunities for upselling

You could then ask questions that would lead to significantly more sales. Begin by asking questions the man should have considered. For instance:

- Do you need a plate to cover the marks on the ceiling left by the light fixture you are replacing?
- Is your ladder adequate – tall and strong enough?
- Do you have all of the tools necessary to do this project?

A sale resulting from any of these questions would be significantly larger than the sale of a single drill bit. Just by showing interest in what the man is trying to do could result in a significantly larger sale.

Yet there are people who think that this approach would be intrusive or overbearing. "Just sell them what they want!" So, let's do it their way. The customer buys your bit, takes it home and begins the installation of the ceiling fan. After removing the existing light fixture, they see that there are marks on the ceiling and they need a plate to cover them up. What do they do?

Chapter 8: What's the Problem?

- Climb down the ladder
- Go back to their car
- Drive to the store – hopefully yours and not a competitor's
- Buy a plate
- Drive back home
- Climb the ladder
- Install the plate

How much would you have saved them if you had sold them the plate on their first visit?

To vs. For

When someone buys from you, have you done something *to* them or something *for* them?

Of course you understand you are doing something for them, right? Does everyone in your organization understand that?

You see, one of your fellow employees might question your intentions. "Hey, if he only wants a drill bit, why are you selling him a plate?" That would be a teaching moment and, after all, the single most important function purpose of sales is to teach. Sometimes you need to do some internal teaching.

You are doing something for your customer when you ask questions like the one above.

Have you ever gone to the store and returned home only to realize you had forgotten something? The one thing you forgot may have been the most important element for your project so you would need to immediately go all the way back to the store, purchase the item, return home and then begin your project.

Don't you wish someone at the store would have asked you about your purchase and offered some alternatives or additions?

Besides, asking a simple question could result in your satisfying your ultimate customer, the stakeholder. The six most profitable words in history may be, "Would you like fries with that?" McDonalds realized that they had an investment in the customer standing at the counter.

The Customer is Usually Wrong

All of their marketing, advertising, community involvement and a host of other efforts had focused on causing that person to come into their store. Whatever they purchased in addition to what they initially ordered would be more profitable than their original order because the marketing expense, known as acquisition cost, had already been covered.

Be sensitive to the concept of acquisition costs. This will help you sell more profitably for your organization and, more importantly, it can be used to help your buyers increase the profitability of theirs. By the time you engage a prospect for the first time, how much has already been invested in that encounter? Your marketing expense is an investment in creating the opportunity. The time you spent preparing for the encounter and scheduling the meeting need to be factored in as well.

In the fast food industry, causing someone to visit one of their outlets is expensive. Why not decide that the experience will be as profitable as possible?

What are the criteria your ultimate customer has established? Greater revenue, greater profit and more market share. Did those six words meet those requirements for McDonalds?

Now, what can you do for your buyers to help them increase their sales on each encounter with their buyers?

A Morrison's Cafeteria employed a young man who was physically handicapped and had a learning disorder. His job was to stand behind the shelves of desserts and keep them pushed in the direction of the customer. As each customer approached, he would ask (with an obvious speech impediment and a smile), "Would you like a nice desert today?" Sales of those after-dinner treat skyrocketed. First of all, most patrons appreciated the fact that the young man was out trying to succeed despite some severe handicaps. Some realized Morrison's deserved some extra business for giving the man a chance. At the heart of the process was a simple "ask."

> It's amazing what people will tell you and give you if you just ask

It is amazing what people will tell you and it is amazing what they will give you if you just ask.

The Next Level

In our hardware store example, you would be the teacher. It would be time to take the customer's education to the next level. You would accomplish this by asking about capabilities he might not know. You're the expert, remember.

You could ask about a rheostat to replace the wall switch. With this device the man could have infinite control over the speed of the fan rather than the three or four options offered by the traditional pull chain. He may not know such a device exists. Since this is a male customer, you could ask, "How about a remote control rheostat?" Remote controls are adult male pacifiers – we can't seem to get enough of them. "You can lay in bed at night and drive your wife crazy adjusting the fan!"

Just by asking the man what outcome he was seeking, all of these sales opportunities opened up. In addition, you would be able to anticipate and solve problems the customer would be unaware of and would inevitably face later.

Think **outcome**. What is your customer trying to accomplish – what outcome do they want? They may order from you by nomenclature or part number, they may give you specific detailed instructions and still not be asking for the best alternative. When you take their order, arve you doing something for them or something to them?

In the final stages of flipping a house, I decided to install a refrigerator with an icemaker. This was an older house that had never had an icemaker before so I would need to run a water line to where the fridge would be sitting. The house had galvanized plumbing and if you have ever worked with it you know it is a knuckle-busting job, especially with older pipes. Some pipes might break in the process and joints might be frozen – but I was determined.

I devoted a Saturday to installing the water line. Early that morning I went down to the basement with a pencil, some paper and a tape measure. I carefully sketched a diagram of what the system would look like and made my materials list.

LaVista Ace Hardware was close by so I approached a seasoned sales professional. "I need a piece of half-inch galvanized pipe three feet four inches long, threaded on each end; another piece of half-inch galvanized two feet one inch long threaded on each end; a tee connector, a reducer, a shut-off valve and twelve feet of copper tubing.

The sales professional studied me for a minute and then asked, "What are you trying to do – put in an icemaker?"

Stunned, I nodded.

"You don't need most of that stuff." Then he introduced me to a saddle valve and taught me how it worked. I had never heard of it. "You turn off the water, clamp this on your pipe, drill one hole right here, connect the tubing and turn the water back on."

I had planned to spend the entire day Saturday in the basement installing the water line. I had already planned to call a plumber on Monday to straighten out the mess I had made on Saturday. Instead, I was done with the job in forty-five minutes and at a considerably lower cost.

How did this happen? He listened. Then he asked what for him was an obvious question based on his knowledge and experience. Asking questions and listening can bring avalanches of information over to your side of the table.

About the time of this project, AT&T had looked at a couple of my ideas for modifying some of their electronic equipment. Seeing value, they applied for and received patents for my modifications. AT&T held the patent, of course, but my initials were on them. What does this mean? While I knew a lot about electronics, I was virtually clueless when it came to plumbing.

The same is true for you. You have expertise and experience in your specialty. Use it. Capitalize on it. Do something for your buyer/customer so they will not be wrong.

Respect But Don't Obey Credentials

Don't let the diplomas and plaques hanging on the wall intimidate you. The person who earned them knows a lot about their area of expertise and they have been recognized by others for their efforts. They deserve your respect. When it comes to your area of expertise, <u>you</u> are the authority.

And don't let their experience in buying what you sell distract you either. One of the favorite tactics of some elder buyers is to say something like, "Son, I was buying these when you were still in diapers." The intent of this approach is for them to position themselves as the authority.

When you think about that approach, it does not make much sense. What you are selling probably did not exist when you were still in diapers. The capabilities, functionality and other aspects of your offering have evolved over the years. Has your contact kept up?

Even the ultimate is customer, the stakeholder, is usually wrong, as we have seen.

If the adage is true that everyone has customers, does the ultimate customer have customers as well?

CHAPTER NINE: WHAT ABOUT INTERNAL CUSTOMERS?

Do you treat others in your organization like customers?

It was a great concept. The idea was that you would treat people inside the organization the same way you would treat people outside. Like many other of the other great concepts, it had a shelf life and we soon moved on to something else.

Maybe it's time for a fresh look at the ideas of internal customers.

Who Is the Ultimate Customer's Customer?

Everybody has customers. Politicians refer to them as voters. Classroom teachers find themselves with a new customer base at the beginning of each school year. A surgeon has an unusually introspective look at their customers.

So the stakeholder who is seen as the ultimate customer must also have customers – who are they? Everyone else in their organization. Now we have come full circle. As salespeople we focus on satisfying the ultimate customer by increasing revenue, increasing profits and increasing market share. We did that by satisfying the buyers who do business with our accounts.

The Ultimate Customer Must Sell

If the leader begins the day by using a demeaning approach to lecture the employees about what a sorry job they're doing, how will those people treat the first few customers they encounter? Not well. They will want – or need – to take out their frustrations on someone. So the first victim to cross their path will likely receive the brunt of their feelings.

The Customer is Usually Wrong

A client used to begin his day by admonishing "the girls down in customer service". His service team was all female, unusually professional with high work ethics and their call center was on the same floor as the CEOs office. Still, he thought the way to kick start good relationships with them was to chastise them daily. This was how he treated "the girls down in customer service". The first customer each of them encountered each morning had to deal with the mindset of "the girls".

Contrast that to many retailers who begin their day with a pep rally. They cheer, they move around and when the first customer who enters the store is greeted energetically.

The Publix grocery store in my neighborhood has this nailed. Every employee I see greets me, asks if they can help and smiles.

It is important to keep morale high. That does not mean that "every day is a holiday and every meal is a banquet." What it means is that people recognize that what they are spending their lives doing is at least meaningful – but preferable <u>valuable</u> – to someone else. For younger generations, this can be a deal-breaker. If they do not feel what they are doing is meaningful, they will move on to another opportunity.

The concept of motivation deserves some study. When asked if I'm a motivational speaker my reply is yes as long as we are using the same definition of motivation.

Motivation is the combination of education and opportunity.

Remove either of those two elements and motivation quickly turns into frustration.

Suppose you were educated at Julliard school of music as a concert pianist but you had no access to a piano. Would you be motivated or frustrated? Your education without opportunity would be discouraging, wouldn't it?

Now suppose someone gave you a grand piano but you did not know how to play it. When people came to your home they would remark on what a beautiful instrument it is. People in the know would tell you that it is one of the finest produced and has a hauntingly wonderful tone. Would you feel frustrated that you could not utilize such a gift?

Chapter 9: What About Internal Customers?

Everyone in your organization contributes to its success. Your ultimate customer, the leader, has a responsibility to maximize the contribution of each individual.

As a minimum, what does the internal customer need: education or opportunity? An employee who is underperforming probably needs education. The employee who is the best-in-class in their area probably needs the opportunity to grow to the next level. They may not realize it, but if you present them with a challenge to go to the next level in most cases they will rise to it and everyone will benefit from the results.

> **Motivation is the combination of education and opportunity**

This about this for a moment. Who was the person who was most instrumental in making you the success that you are today? Was it someone who made it so easy for you that you could not possibly fail? Or, was it someone who stretched you beyond your perceived limitations?

Now, go be that type of leader.

After ten years as an entry-level technician at AT&T a gentleman called me into his office and said, "I see more in you than you see in yourself. I'm going to get you out of here." He was looking at a good employee, one who came to work every day, worked hard, took on extra assignments and even made a few improvements in the technologies. He was announcing that he was willing to lose this employee because it would be best for the employee but not for him.

When he stated that he was sending me to sales, I said no. I could not speak to strangers, let alone speak in public. I did not have a college degree. In fact, I did not even own a suit – a requirement for a sales position. I was his internal customer, I had planned to retire as a technician at AT&T but as we know, the customer is usually wrong.

> **With the right education and opportunity anyone can be a superstar**

He leaned across his desk, made solid eye contact and said, "I want you to try this for me." As a result, my first full year as an account executive I was named top salesperson out of a universe of 1,100 salespeople.

Which of your internal customers is a budding superstar? You may have a fork lift operator who believes that's all he can do. Are they wrong? Could they actually be a warehouse supervisor or manager? Maybe you have a clerical person who is your best paper pusher and their pride in their ability to do their job as well as they do has them convinced they're at the pinnacle of their success and achievement. They are probably wrong.

With the right education and opportunity I believe anyone can be a superstar.

Teach Them Why

Internal customers will sometimes do the wrong thing for the right reason. At least they think it's the right reason. Internal customers, after all, are not immune from being wrong.

The most common example of this is the rank-and-file employee who thinks you are overcharging for your products and services. If they think that way and they have customer contact responsibilities, they will communicate their perspective to your customers – both internal and external.

A software engineer may think their company is overcharging for their program because after all it is "only some code and a CD". For the engineer, it is not that big of a deal. For the user, however, the program may be saving them hours and dollars while improving the overall quality of their product or service. It is worth a lot to them. The perceived value to the user is greater than the perceived value of the programmer.

A friend did me a big favor and would not let me pay him back. I knew he wanted a Mont Blanc pen so I decided to give him one. At the pen store the person behind the counter tried to steer me to less expensive pens. I had to force him to even take the Mont Blanc out of the case. Finally he put it on the counter and said, "I would never pay that for it."

Employees can overtly and inadvertently inflict their value system on the folks who buy our products and services.

A client in San Jose had to move because their building was being demolished. AT&T would oversee the communications and coordinate their services with the local operating company, some cable contractors, the architect, the builder and others. Problems arose as the project progressed. In order to have the equipment delivered on time a box of

Chapter 9: What About Internal Customers?

cigars was sent to a truck terminal manager in Denver. In order to have enough cable, a weekend was spent driving around San Jose and sending food and soft drinks down manholes. At one point, the avocado farmer next door to the new location had to be approached for permission to bring a truck across his farm road. This was done in defiance of his huge sign that read "TRESSPASSERS WILL BE SHOT". Many other obstacles were addressed one at a time and it looked like the move would go on schedule.

The objective was that the customer would close down on a Friday at the old location and open up Monday morning in the new one. There would be no sleeping over the weekend as the services were installed and tested.

On the Monday before the move the customer in San Jose called me in Atlanta and was chewing me out so strongly a Marine would have been embarrassed. Tuesday morning I was in his office and he continued his tirade.

"You sold me a 400 switch and all we will ever need is a 100! You sold me a bill if goods! I am not going to pay for a 400, I will only pay for a 100. If you can get a 100 out here by Friday, that's fine. I'm not paying for the 400!" (NOTE: I am omitting many words that he used for emphasis!)

Once he had vented I said, "Let's go back nine months. Nine months ago when we started this project you said one of your major problems was your inability to back bill your clients for phone calls you made on their behalf. Your analysis showed that if you could recover that revenue it would actually pay for the new switch."

As I talked he began to relax. The color came back in his face.

I continued, "The 400 switch has the ability to capture that information in real time; the 100 cannot offer that. So, you can have a 400 for 'free' because it will pay for itself or you can have a 100 and you'll have to pay our ridiculous prices." (Humor helps to diffuse anger, sometimes.)

He immediately began apologizing which was appreciated but unnecessary. Was he under a lot of pressure? Of course he was. Construction alone would have been a major stressor but then, added to that, the pressures of moving an entire office, training employees on some new protocols – it was enough to drive anyone crazy.

The Customer is Usually Wrong

Soon we were talking as we had in the past so I asked, "What brought this up?"

"Your installer. Your installer came out here and said, 'Boy, some salesperson sold you a bill of goods. You will never need the capacity of the 400; the 100 is all you need!'"

Was the installer trying to do the right thing for this customer? Of course he was. From his perspective the customer had bought far more capacity than he would ever need. In the world of installation overcapacity equals overselling.

Perception- Your Lens

The installer was trying to do the right thing for the customer but, in the end, managed to create greater stress for the user and for the salesperson. This was not intentional so what caused this behavior to appear to be acceptable – even preferable – for the installer? To understand this, you must first understand how people see the world.

Everyone sees the world through two lens: Education and Experience.

Education is everything you have learned formally and informally. It includes your educational level as well as the article you read yesterday. With so much information flowing intensely and being easily accessible, you are being exposed to more learning now than you can absorb. You have become selective in how you use your educational time. You have to, you know.

> Everyone sees the world through two lens: education and experience

And so does everyone else. Everyone chooses to focus on the information that can best help them accomplish their personal and professional objectives. While you have learned how improve your performance in your areas of interest, so have others. This does not indicate that anyone is right or wrong; it is only a reflection of their areas of focus.

In the scenario above, the installer had learned about the capacity of the equipment in addition to the thousands of details he had to learn in order to make the equipment operate optimally. The salesperson had learned how to cost justify the equipment in order to improve the bottom line of the user's organization. The salesperson would not know how to make the equipment work; they only knew what it was capable of accomplishing.

Experience is any event in your life that affects the way you think.

These can be positive or negative experiences. We learn more from falling down and then picking ourselves back up again than we do from walking upright. Every sales call is a potential learning experience. By conducting post-call critiques we can benefit greatly from each call. Win, lose or draw, stop and evaluate as many details of the call as you can. What did you do well – and will repeat in the future? What did you do that did not go well and will be something you are careful not to do in the future?

Many sales professionals record their sales calls so they can hear what their customers heard.

From time to time everyone in your organization needs to be reminded of what you are doing for the people who are paying you for your offering. So we are back to "TO" and "FOR" again.

It may be easier than you think for some of the people on your team to begin thinking you are doing something <u>to</u> your buyers rather than <u>for</u> your buyers, like the installer did. What drives that thinking?

The way they see things through their two lens, Education and Experience, are different from yours and each of yours may be significantly different from how your buyers see the world. People who want quality do not mind paying extra for what they want but they can resent having to pay anything at all for something they do not want. This can be difficult for some people to understand.

A retired bank president needed to have his wife's home computer repaired so he called in a local technician. After some diagnostics, the tech found that the motherboard was bad and was able to install a used board he had on hand, thus saving the retired couple some money – maybe $50. This was an affluent couple for whom $50 is less than they pay for dinner each night. Only a few days later the replacement motherboard failed and the wife was, once again, without the use of her computer. When the couple learned that the tech had installed a used board just to save a few dollars, they were angry and never used the tech again.

The Customer is Usually Wrong

Uptime and privacy for this couple were more important than money. Having the second failure and having the tech in their house twice was something they did not want happening <u>to</u> them. So while the tech thought he was doing something <u>for</u> them, based on his perspective, he was actually doing something <u>to</u> them.

EDUCATE! EVERYONE IS A TEACHER AND EVERYONE IS A STUDENT

It's simple but it isn't easy.

The simplicity of all of this is apparent: raise your revenue and profit and increase your market share.

It is simple but it's not easy. There are enough obstacles and barriers for anyone to find ready excuses for not meeting the expectations of their ultimate customer. Excuses are easy; achievement brings results. You want to be known as a person of accomplishment, not a purveyor of excuses.

Therefore, when your president, CEO or other stakeholder says that the way to satisfy them is to raise your revenues, profits and market share, that becomes your objective. You want to satisfy your ultimate customer for multiple reasons, not the least of which is your own personal career advancement. You will look for ways to <u>better</u> satisfy – not <u>simply</u> satisfy – them. You want to be a winner.

Another myth is that everyone loves a winner. Losers do not love winners; they resent them. Your success is going to make them look bad. So what is the secret for making your ultimate customer happy?

Make it as easy as possible for everyone to please your ultimate customer. Even your detractors need to be sold on the idea of pleasing your ultimate customer.

This is especially true if you are in sales. Think about it.

Let's say your ultimate customer has determined that one way to increase profits is to lower costs by reducing headcount. And, let's say, this is being done because automation has increased productivity in a way that makes this a viable option. Meanwhile, some disgruntled employees think they "have to do the work of two people now" and use that as an excuse for missing due dates.

Chapter 9: What About Internal Customers?

When a due date is missed, who will hear from the buyer first? Of course their salesperson will be the first person on their list. If they cannot contact you for whatever reason, the next person will be your supervisor and then they will make their way up the chain. Notice, they will go *up* the chain all the way to your ultimate customer if necessary; they will not go *down* the chain to the disgruntled employees.

> Excuses are easy; achievement brings results. Most people desire to be achievers.

Or, suppose the fine folks in accounting have determined that a price increase is necessary in order to maintain the margin set by your ultimate customer. As a salesperson you will be the one to deliver the news to the buyer, won't you? The buyer is not going to ask your accounting folks about the changes in raw material costs, utility fee increases or any other factors. Then, if you cannot cost justify the new pricing, they may go up in your organization but, more likely, they will begin shopping around.

Remember, everyone is in sales. Make it easy for those "other salespeople" to meet or exceed your buyer's demands in order to satisfy your ultimate customer.

Let's begin with the disgruntled employees. Some people in this category just don't like change, some are looking for any excuse to complain and some are just obnoxious. They all lack knowledge and the single, most important function of sales is to teach. Make it easy for them to learn why meeting your buyer's demand is in their best interest.

For instance, if they think they will be doing the work of two people, they will still be doing some work, right? What would it take for the work they do to be directed to your buyers? If they are going to do anything they might as well do it for your buyers rather than someone else's.

One of the most effective ways to accomplish this is to humanize your buyer in the mind of the disgruntled employee. If the employee could see your buyer as someone who needs help would they react differently?

> Help may be the most powerful word in the English language

Help may be the most powerful word in the English language. It will stop men in Armani suits on the streets in Manhattan. It will cause an otherwise disinterested party to engage with stranger.

The Customer is Usually Wrong

When travelling, how many times have you seen opportunities to help fellow travelers? Maybe it is the elderly person trying to put their suitcase in the overhead bin. Maybe it's a mother trying to herd several kids. If anyone asks you for help, will you come through? Almost always, you will respond positively to request for help.

So will the disgruntled employee.

How you approach them can make a huge difference in whether or not you will be successful. Rather than, "Mike, my customer needs their order filled right away," and hearing Mike respond, "Get in line with everybody else!" try this approach. "Mike, Bob Smith from Acme Widgets just called. They will need to send their production people home for the day without pay if they don't have their order. Do you have any ideas about how we could help them out?"

Examine that question and you'll see some of the magic. First of all it is Bob Smith, not "my customer". We have humanized him. Your customer is your problem. Secondly, we associate him with a major account. Then we make the humanization relative to the disgruntled employee. Employees understand losing a day's pay. Then, in our "help" question we use the plural pronoun: we. We are not laying everything on the employee; we are including ourselves.

The principle here is what Robert Woodruff, Chairman of Coca-Cola, is quoted as saying: "It's amazing what you can accomplish when you don't care who gets the credit."

REAL WORLD EXAMPLE

As an entry-level technician for AT&T one of my assignments was to work the trouble desk for what was then the highest-speed data service we offered. (It was 7200 bps – don't laugh!) The service was so costly that we offered it on a shared basis and as a result two distribution centers for major catalog companies, like Amazon, used it. One transmitted data in the morning and the other in the afternoon.

One morning Client A called and said the service was not working. I rolled an equipment cabinet over to the access point and began setting up for the initial diagnostics. Before I could even connect the test equipment he called again wanting a status. He was anxious. As I isolated the problem he called two more times. On his fourth call of the morning I explained that a piece of equipment that was located in a manhole

Chapter 9: What About Internal Customers?

between his location and mine had apparently failed and a technician would be dispatched immediately.

A couple of hours later we had the service restored so I called Client A to tell him his service was up and running and to gain his undying appreciation. To my surprise he said, "Okay, I'll check it in a little while."

Confused, I asked, "You were so anxious when you called in – what has changed?"

"We download our orders in the morning and our warehouse people spend the day picking them and we ship them out." He paused, "When there are no orders thee is no work so we sent everyone home without pay."

As a technician I did not understand distribution, order fulfillment or the economies of shipping full trucks versus partially-loaded trucks. I did understand losing a day's pay.

That's not the end of the story. It bugged me that the diagnostics had taken so long. So when there was time I began devising ways to make the various components more accessible. A few false starts later, I submitted an employee suggestion based on my contraption, someone from Bell Laboratories came to Atlanta and looked at it and before long the design was patented and the real components were produced by some people who knew what they were doing. Their rig looked a lot better than my contraption.

INVOLVE YOUR INTERNAL CUSTOMERS AND EXPECT MAGIC

The point here is that I am not exceptional. You have people in all job titles in your organization who can devise creative processes and tools that will help you serve your buyers better. When they succeed, they will experience a feeling of accomplishment that cannot be gained any other way.

After the initial, "Can't be done," "Never done that before," and "Are you crazy?" remarks, encourage them to get involved. Offer to help them in any way you can. You are not assigning blame and responsibility; you're offering to be on their team. Keep in mind you are doing something *for* them, not *to* them. You are creating an event that could be pivotal in their personal and professional development. It's not okay to say, "You will thank me later," but it is okay to think it!

What about those folks in accounting? When they proclaim that a price increase is needed in order to achieve the margin requirements of your ultimate customer, what do you do? They will not have to face the buyer. They do not have to explain to your contact why they will have to pay more while receiving the same product or service, you will. After all, when we pay more shouldn't we get more they will ask?

Your buyer may use the price increase as a reason to go shopping. When your competitors do not participate in price increases at the same time you do, the buyer needs a reason to stay with you or they will leave. You have some reasons, of course, like your ability to understand their unique needs better than a new vendor would. And you have a legacy you can build on like the times you came through for them in a bind.

Still, your contact may need some hard numbers and you don't have them. Accountants like to play with numbers so involve them.

Humanize the buyer. In the accountant's mind, the buyer may be just a line number on a spreadsheet somewhere. You know what your buyer is going to say and how they are going to react. Ask your accounting person for some pointers.

Begin by talking about your contact. Whenever it is appropriate, introduce your contact to the accounting person using their first and last name. Afterwards, use your contact's first name only. "John Smith at Acme Widgets and I were talking and John laid it out for me. He really wants to continue doing business with us but he has to convince his superiors that we are worth the higher price. What ideas do you have that would help John?"

Notice we are using the magic four-letter word again: help. This time we attach it as close to the account as possible. The inference here is that the accounting person needs to help John.

"What are some other ways we might be able to help John?" This question can cause the accounting person to think outside the box. Notice the use of the plural pronoun!

Accounting people are not really known for being creative. However, when it comes to managing and manipulating numbers, they are as creative as anyone. Maybe they can suggest some creative payment terms or even delay the price increase in order to "help John." They understand things like "time value of money" and "discounted cash flow". Perhaps one of those obscure financial principles could be used.

If they come up empty or are unwilling to help, use a phrase like, "John has been a really loyal buyer. It a shame we are leaving him in a lurch here."

If necessary, turn up the heat. "Do you know what accounting tricks the competition must be using?" Infer that the competitor's accounting people are smarter than your accounting people. Accountants are not necessarily competitive. However, their desire for accuracy is phenomenal. Use that.

Your Team of Winners

When the Tart Group posed the question, 88% of the people polled put themselves in the top 25% of physically fit people. That is statistically impossible but it drives home an important point: people are crazy about themselves.

Capitalize on the idea that everyone wants to play on a winning team.

ANSWERS

When I was in school I always liked those text books that had the answers in the back of the book. So I am placing the answers here in the back of this book. You might think of this as the Cliff Notes or, more accurately, as the Chuck Notes.

This is a place where you can review the concepts in the book. If your organization has made this an assigned reading and you either don't want to read the entire book or you waited until the last minute, here are the highlights. To best capitalize on the ideas in "The Customer Is Usually Wrong", you really need to understand the context around the ideas.

In other words, read the book. Then you can use this chapter as a refresher.

The single, most important function of sales is to teach.

Why Customers Are Wrong

- Customers are wrong because they are ignorant
- They are ignorant because salespeople have not taken the time to teach them
- Salespeople have not taken the time to teach their customers because
    - They do not know they are supposed to teach
    - They do not know how to teach
    - They have not taken the time to determine what the customer needs to learn
    - Their leaders have not provided the training and/or incentive for them to take the time to teach
    - They think the customer is always right

The Customer is Not the Customer

- Salespeople typically engage buyers, not customers
- Buyers implement purchasing decisions
- Purchasers make purchasing decisions
    - Purchasers' decisions are based on their best understanding of what you sell
    - Purchasers my not have the latest information about your capabilities
    - Purchasers lack important information when they are ignorant
    - They are ignorant when they have not been taught
- Salespeople do not teach purchasers when they stop at the buyer level
- Purchasers determine solutions
    - For solving problems
    - For achieving objectives
- Problems and objectives are the responsibility of the leadership team
- Leadership teams often concentrate on symptoms instead of problems
- Leadership teams deserve to be taught how to look past symptoms and find solutions
- ***The single, most important function of sales is to teach***
- Solving the problems of the organization that pays for your product or service may not satisfy your ultimate customer
- Your ultimate customer is usually on the same payroll as you are
- Even ultimate customers have customers

Most Customers Don't Know What They Want

- Buying decisions are made based on available knowledge
- Buyers usually lack the best, most current knowledge
- Teaching the buyer is a function of sales and a function of marketing

- Competitive comparisons are based on their understanding of the capabilities of your product and/or service

Buyers Are Not Customers

- Find the person who determines what will be purchased
- Purchasing agents make wise buying decisions, not wise purchasing decisions
- Determine which individual or department in the buyer's organization will benefit most from what you sell

Everyone Buys and Sells

- Focus on pleasing your stakeholders
    - o Are they the ultimate customers?
    - o They can only be satisfied when sales are up
    - o Sales will be up when buyers place more orders with you
- Internal customers need to be taught

AFTERWORD

THE MOST POWERFUL WORD IN THE ENGLISH LANGUAGE

You have probably heard that the most powerful word in the English language is love. It may have been at one time but the overuse and misuse of the word has rendered it weak.

A friend of my wife came over to our house. At the front door she said, "Oh, I love your hair." Once inside she said, "I love what you have done here!" Later she would confide in my wife by beginning, "I'm not sure I still love my husband but…"

Maybe she would love her husband if he had a new front door or new slip covers?

What's Love Got To Do With It?

So the word love has been compromised. The Captain and Tennille taught my generation that love will keep us together only to have Tina Turner question that assumption.

The apostle Paul listed a number of virtues and concluded by stating that the greatest of them was love.

Who are we to argue?

In fact, the most powerful word in sales – and in my estimation the English language – is help. It will stop men in Armani suits on the streets of Manhattan. It will cause strangers to alter their plans.

Few people will not respond positively to a genuine request for help. One of the reasons is that we realize that at some point all of us will need help. The few that refuse to help anyone at any time have deep-seated mental or emotional issues. We are probably better off without their help!

So, look for opportunities to help. Whether you are in sales or any other profession, part of your job description is to help.

If you are retired there must be many ways you could help. You have much to teach. Share your wisdom. Wisdom is the combination of education and experience. Much of what you have learned is obsolete – we live in a changing world. However, your life experiences, those lessons that only be learned through practice, never go out of style. When your past experiences can be combined with new knowledge lives can be altered.

There is a story of a janitor mopping the floor of the science lab at the university late at night. He was surprised to find a young student diligently experimenting with various chemicals. When asked, the student proudly said, "I'm trying to invent a universal solvent, something that will dissolve anything." The janitor continued to clean the floor and asked, "What will you put it in?"

When we look for opportunities to help we find they are more plentiful than we imagined.

As a frequent traveler, I see multiple occasions on each trip. Travelling is difficult enough for those of us who know the ropes. We also see the ropes changing frequently. So, when the occasional traveler crosses our path, how do we respond? Too many of us see them as rookies who are intruding on our familiar turf. Instead, taking an attitude helping them can make travelling more rewarding rather than more cumbersome. So they don't realize their bag should go in the overhead bin wheels or handle first. Rather than snicker, sneer or complain, teach them. If they are intelligent enough to navigate the airport maze and run the TSA gauntlet, they are smart enough to learn.

According to a recent survey by The Grid, the second-worst passengers on an airplane are seat recliners. With the reduction in space at an all-time high, the recliner realizes a few inches in additional space while robbing the person behind them of nearly two feet. People who travel infrequently do not realize their slight recline paralyzes the person behind them, preventing them from shifting or crossing their legs.

Mothers travelling with children need – and deserve – our help. Let the elderly have the available taxi and wait for the next one. The celebratory foursome at the restaurant can have the next table while we wait for another.

Once you become sensitive to and capitalize the opportunities to help, you will feel better when your head hits the pillow each night.

www.ingramcontent.com/pod-product-compliance
Lightning Source LLC
Chambersburg PA
CBHW051816170526
45167CB00005B/2039